This book belongs to

Thank You

Thank you to all my family and friends, including the staff at Lindamood-Bell and Gander Publishing, for providing us with their favorite family recipes. I appreciate your love of food and your love of children.

The proceeds from this book go to the Rhett Bell Scholarship Foundation, a public nonprofit 509(a) foundation formed to help children and adults learn to their potential. Thank you for helping us give the gift of learning.

A special thanks to Christy Bonetti for the original art work. Being Bib's granddaughter and watching Rhett grow from a little boy to a handsome teenager, Christy put her heart and soul into this project. Thank you.

Nanci Bell

COPYRIGHT © 2003 Rhett Bell Scholarship Foundation

Gander Publishing
412 Higuera Street, Suite 200
San Luis Obispo, CA 93401
805-541-5523 • 800-554-5523

All rights reserved. No part of this material shall be reproduced or transmitted in any form or by any means, electronic or mechanical, including photocopying, recording, or by any information or retrieval system, without prior written permission from the Publisher. Printed in the U.S.A.

ISBN 0-945856-31-8

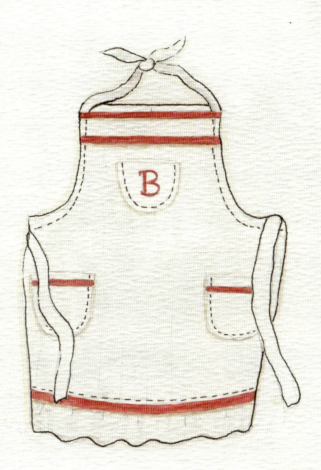

Table of Contents

Appetizers 9

Salads 17

Soups 25

Veggies and Side Dishes 33

Weeknight Dinners 43

Main Dishes 51

Desserts 63

Baked Goods and Sweets 69

Breakfast Goodies 85

Appetizers

ARTICHOKE DIP

Alison Bell, San Luis Obispo, California
(Bib's Granddaughter)

This is a quick and snappy appetizer that will be a hit at any party or event. Serve it on crackers or sourdough bread.

8 oz. cream cheese, softened
1/2 c. sour cream
1 can green chilies, chopped
1 jar marinated artichoke hearts, slightly chopped
1/2 c. shredded parmesan cheese

Mix all ingredients. Bake covered or uncovered at 350° for 25-30 minutes.

California-Style Guacamole

Chantelle Cappa, New York, New York

As the only Californian in the New York office, I am required to bring guacamole to all festivities, even in the dead of winter!

3 California Hass avocados, ripe
1/2 c. of coarsely chopped cilantro
1/2 c. of chopped yellow onion
1 to 2 tomatoes, cut into small cubes
1 clove of garlic, pressed or minced
2 tsp. salt
dash of garlic powder
juice of 1 lime

Slice avocados vertically into halves. Scoop the avocado out of the skin and place in a large bowl. Save the pits for later. Add cilantro, onion, tomatoes, garlic, garlic powder, and salt, and stir. Squeeze the lime juice and stir (use another lime if there is not enough juice). Add 2 of the avocado pits in the guacamole to help keep it green and mix. Garnish with cilantro and diced tomatoes. Enjoy!

Kevin's Salmon Spread

KEVIN FOSTER, DEERFIELD, ILLINOIS

This is a recipe that is quick and easy, and can be made a day ahead of your upcoming party.

smoked Alaskan salmon
1 pkg. of cream cheese, softened
garlic powder to taste
salt to taste
Worcestershire sauce, 2-3 dashes

Mix ingredients together and add more garlic powder to taste, if desired. Let sit overnight for the best flavor. Serve on crackers or toast points.

ASPARAGUS BUNDLES

Christi Bonetti, Monterey, California
(Bib's Granddaughter)

This dish looks great at Christmas dinner with the asparagus wrapped up like a little package. It's also nice at an Easter brunch when the asparagus are in season.

1 bunch asparagus
2 bell peppers, roasted
Prosciutto ham slices
Fontina cheese

Put red bell peppers in a pan and roast at 350° until the skin starts to blister on all sides. Put peppers in a paper bag until cool. Peel the skin from peppers. Steam the asparagus until just cooked and let cool. Then cut peppers into 1/2 inch strips. Wrap the asparagus in the Prosciutto with a slice of Fontina cheese (I usually bundle 3 stalks together). Next wrap the bundle with a bow of red pepper strip. Heat or microwave until cheese starts to melt.

prosciutto with cheese inside tied with roasted bell pepper

WENDY'S IN-A-HURRY APPETIZER

WENDY COOK, SAN LUIS OBISPO, CALIFORNIA

Be sure to leave yourself plenty of time for this one; it takes a good five minutes to pull it together. It's always a big hit—better bring two!

1 block of cream cheese
soy sauce
sesame seeds
box of Wheat Thins

Put the cream cheese on a serving platter and stab it a bunch of times with a fork (I actually use a metal skewer). Slowly pour soy sauce (I use the spicy Kikkoman Tabasco version) into the holes and on top of the cream cheese. Toast the sesame seeds in a pan with cooking spray until just slightly brown. Sprinkle on top of cream cheese.
Serve with crackers.

ARTICHOKE NIBBLES

DOT RENZ, TRES PINOS, CALIFORNIA
(BIB'S DAUGHTER)

A little preparation, but mmmm good.

2 6 oz. jars marinated artichoke hearts
1 small onion, chopped
1 clove garlic, minced
4 eggs
1/4 c. fine dry bread crumbs
1/4 tsp. salt
1/4 tsp. each pepper, oregano, and liquid hot pepper
2 c. (1/2 lb.) sharp cheddar cheese, shredded
2 Tbsp. minced parsley

Drain marinade from one jar of artichoke hearts into a frying pan. Drain the other jar and chop all artichokes; set aside. Add onion and garlic to pan and saute until limp, about 5 minutes. In a bowl, beat the eggs with a fork. Add crumbs, salt, pepper, oregano, and hot pepper. Stir in the saute mixture, artichokes, parsley and the cheese. Turn into a greased 7X11" (or larger) baking pan. Bake at 325° for 30 minutes, or until set when lightly touched. Let cool in pan, then cut into 1" squares. Serve cold or reheat in the pan for 10-12 minutes.

Salads

Chinese Chicken Salad

Misa Terahira, Saratoga, California

This is a great recipe and a guaranteed success
at any luncheon, dinner, or potluck.

1 head of cabbage, finely shredded
1 lb. chicken, boiled and shredded
4 green onions, chopped
1/2 bunch cilantro, chopped
1/2 c. of slivered almonds
1/2 c. of roasted sesame seeds
1 pkg. Top Ramen
1 Tbsp. butter

Dressing:
1/2 c. oil
2 Tbsp. sesame oil
2 Tbsp. soy sauce
1/2 c. sugar
1/4 c. seasoned rice vinegar
1/2 tsp. black pepper

Combine first four ingredients in a large bowl; set aside. Melt the butter in a skillet and brown the almonds. Add the Top Ramen noodles and sesame seeds, then mix in Top Ramen seasoning. Set aside and let the mixture cool. Combine all of the dressing ingredients in a jar and shake vigorously. Mix almonds, sesame seeds, and Top Ramen into the bowl of cabbage, chicken, green onion, and cilantro. Add dressing and toss.

Salad Niçoise

Pilar Dandes, Weston, Florida

This is a classic version of a classic salad, great to serve for a casual dinner with friends.

2 lbs. green beans, trimmed and cut into 1 1/2 inch lengths
2 green peppers, ribs removed and cut into thin rounds
2 c. celery, thinly sliced * 1 pint cherry tomatoes
5 medium red potatoes, cooked, peeled, sliced
21 oz. canned tuna, drained * 2 oz. can flat anchovies, drained
10 black Greek olives * 10 small pimiento stuffed olives
2 Tbsp. fresh basil, chopped * 1 large red onion, thinly sliced
1/4 c. scallions, finely chopped * 1/3 c. parsley, finely chopped
6 hard-boiled eggs, quartered

Dressing:
2 tsp. Dijon mustard * 1 1/2 tsp. salt
6 Tbsp. vegetable oil * 1 tsp. fresh thyme
2 Tbsp. wine vinegar * 6 Tbsp. olive oil * 2 cloves garlic, minced

Combine all of the dressing ingredients in a large jar and shake until well blended. Set aside. Steam beans until tender crisp. Drain. Refresh under cold water. Drain. Place beans, green pepper, celery, tomatoes, and potatoes in a large salad bowl, arranging in a symmetrical pattern. Flake tuna over vegetables. Arrange anchovies on top. Scatter olives and red onions over all. Sprinkle with basil, parsley, and scallions. Garnish with quartered eggs. Toss with dressing and serve.

CHICKEN SALAD WITH POPPY SEEDS

SHANNON KENDALL, INDIANAPOLIS, INDIANA

When the weather is really hot, I love to make this salad for dinner because it tastes so light and refreshing.

4 whole chicken breasts, cooked and torn into bite-size pieces
1 1/2 head of iceberg lettuce
3 green onions, thinly sliced
1 small pkg. sliced almonds, toasted
1 Tbsp. butter
3 oz. Chinese noodles

Dressing:
8 Tbsp. sugar
2 tsp. salt
1 tsp. Accent
1/2 tsp. pepper
8 Tbsp. white vinegar
1 c. salad oil
1/2 c. poppy seeds

Combine first five ingredients in a large bowl; set aside. Combine all of the dressing ingredients in a jar and pour over bowl of salad. Just before serving, add dressing and Chinese noodles, and toss. You may add Mandarin oranges, if desired.

IT'S NOT YOUR MOTHER'S SPINACH SALAD

Terri Mehl, Sacramento, California

This is a fresh little twist on the traditional spinach salad.

2 bunches of spinach, washed and shredded
1 large red onions, thinly sliced
1 can mandarin oranges, drained and chilled
1 c. feta cheese
1 c. Ocean Spray Craisins
1 Tbsp. butter
1/2 c. toasted almonds
1/4 c. Paul Newman Balsamic Vinegarette dressing
1/4 c. orange juice

In a small bowl, whisk the orange juice and salad dressing; set aside. Combine all of the other ingredients in large bowl. Add dressing and toss, then let sit for about 15 minutes before serving. Sprinkle with fresh cracked pepper to taste. Wow!

WHOOTEN FAMILY CRANBERRY SALAD

Stacey Whooten, San Francisco, California

This is great-grandmother Hazel Whooten's recipe and is great to use during the holiday season.

1 c. cranberries, ground up and strained
1 c. apples, ground up and strained
1/2 c. sugar
1 c. whipping cream
1/2 bag small marshmallows

Put cranberries and apples into a large mixing bowl. Add sugar and set aside. In a separate bowl, mix whipping cream until soft to firm peaks form. Fold whipped cream into cranberry and apple mixture. Refrigerate one hour before serving. Top with marshmallows.

Raspberry Jello Salad

Nanci Bell, San Luis Obispo, California

We serve this at every Thanksgiving and Christmas dinner. It is a great recipe! I originally learned how to make this from my stepmother, Nina Netto. She was a great cook and a great stepmother.

2 small pkgs. or 1 large pkg. of raspberry Jello
2 pkgs. of frozen raspberries, in syrup, thawed
2 c. boiling water
2 large bananas, sliced
1 small can crushed pineapple, drained
sour cream, one large container

Dissolve Jello in hot water. Add raspberries, bananas, and pineapple. Put half in mold and refrigerate until it sets. Then add sour cream layer and remaining Jello mixture. Refrigerate. Unmold. It is beautiful and serves 12-18.

Soups

Taco Soup
Dianne Hibbs, Atlanta, Georgia

If you are in a hurry, you can use canned chicken instead of baking and shredding the breasts, or you can leave the chicken out altogether and still have a festive soup.

2 cans Rotell tomatoes
2 cans fiesta corn
2 cans black beans, rinsed and drained
1 pkg. taco seasoning mix
1 pkg. powdered ranch dressing mix
1 large onion, chopped
3 cloves of garlic, minced
3 chicken breasts
3 cans of herbed chicken broth
garnish with Monterey Jack cheese, sour cream, and avocado slices, if desired

Bake and shred the chicken breast and set aside. Chop and saute the onion in a little olive oil. Add everything else to the pot and simmer for one hour. Top with the garnishes of your choice. Serves 10.

Italian Sausage and Tortellini Soup
Jane Miller, San Luis Obispo, California

This is a favorite for cold winter evenings. Hot Italian sausage can be substituted for a little kick.

1 lb. mild Italian sausage, casings removed
1 c. onion, chopped
2 large cloves garlic, sliced
5 c. beef stock or canned broth (chicken broth can be substituted)
2 c. chopped tomatoes or 1 large can diced tomatoes
1 8 oz. can tomato sauce
1 large zucchini, sliced
1 large carrot, thinly sliced
1 medium green bell pepper, diced
1/2 c. dry red wine
2 Tbsp. dried basil
2 Tbsp. dried oregano
8 to 10 oz. fresh cheese tortellini
freshly grated Parmesan cheese

Saute Italian sausage in heavy Dutch oven over medium-high heat until cooked through, about ten minutes. Using a slotted spoon, transfer sausage to large bowl. Pour off all but 1 tbsp. of the drippings from the Dutch oven. Add onion and garlic to Dutch oven and saute until translucent, about 5 minutes. Return sausage to Dutch oven. Add stock, tomatoes, tomato sauce, zucchini, carrot, bell pepper, wine, basil, and oregano. Simmer until vegetables are tender, about 40 minutes. Add tortellini to soup and cook until tender; about 8 minutes. Season soup to taste with salt and pepper. Ladle soup into bowls. Sprinkle with Parmesan and serve with warm bread.

OLD-FASHIONED CROCKPOT CHICKEN SOUP

TERRI MEHL, SACRAMENTO, CALIFORNIA

This was my mom's recipe in the 1950s! It's a nice winter comfort food for the 21st century. Your family and friends may not even know what a crockpot looks like!

2 onions, chopped
2 to 3 carrots, sliced
2 stalks celery, sliced
2 tsp. each salt and white pepper
6 basil leaves, rolled together and chopped
1 sprig fresh thyme, chopped
1/4 c. fresh parsley, chopped
2 lbs. chicken pieces (with or without skin)
3 c. water
3 c. fat-free chicken broth
1 to 2 c.s uncooked noodles

Place everything in your crockpot, except noodles, in the order listed. Cover and cook on Low 8-10 hours (High would be 4-6 hours). One hour before serving, remove chicken and cool slightly. Remove meat from bones and skin from meat. Cut in pieces about the size of the carrots and celery pieces or slightly larger. Return meat to crockpot. Add noodles. Turn to high. Cover and cook one hour. Add or lessen liquid depending on whether or not you like some or lots of broth. Serves 4.

Jan's Veggie Soup

Cornelia Fletcher, Atlanta, Georgia

I love this recipe because it takes about 30 minutes to put together and tastes as if you've been working at it all day! Serve it with some great corn bread muffins and honey butter.

2 lbs. ground beef
2 onion chopped
garlic powder, to taste
2 cans diced tomatoes
2 can whole corn, drained
2 can cream style corn
2 can Veg-All
2 can lima beans (optional)
2 can tomato sauce
2 c. frozen okra (optional)
2 pkgs. McCormick beef stew seasoning to taste

Cook ground beef, onion, and garlic powder. Mix with all the other ingredients and add McCormick seasoning. This gives "the cooked all day flavor." Simmer for 2 minutes.

SHRIMP CHOWDER
Joanne Thorp Leach, Greenfield, California

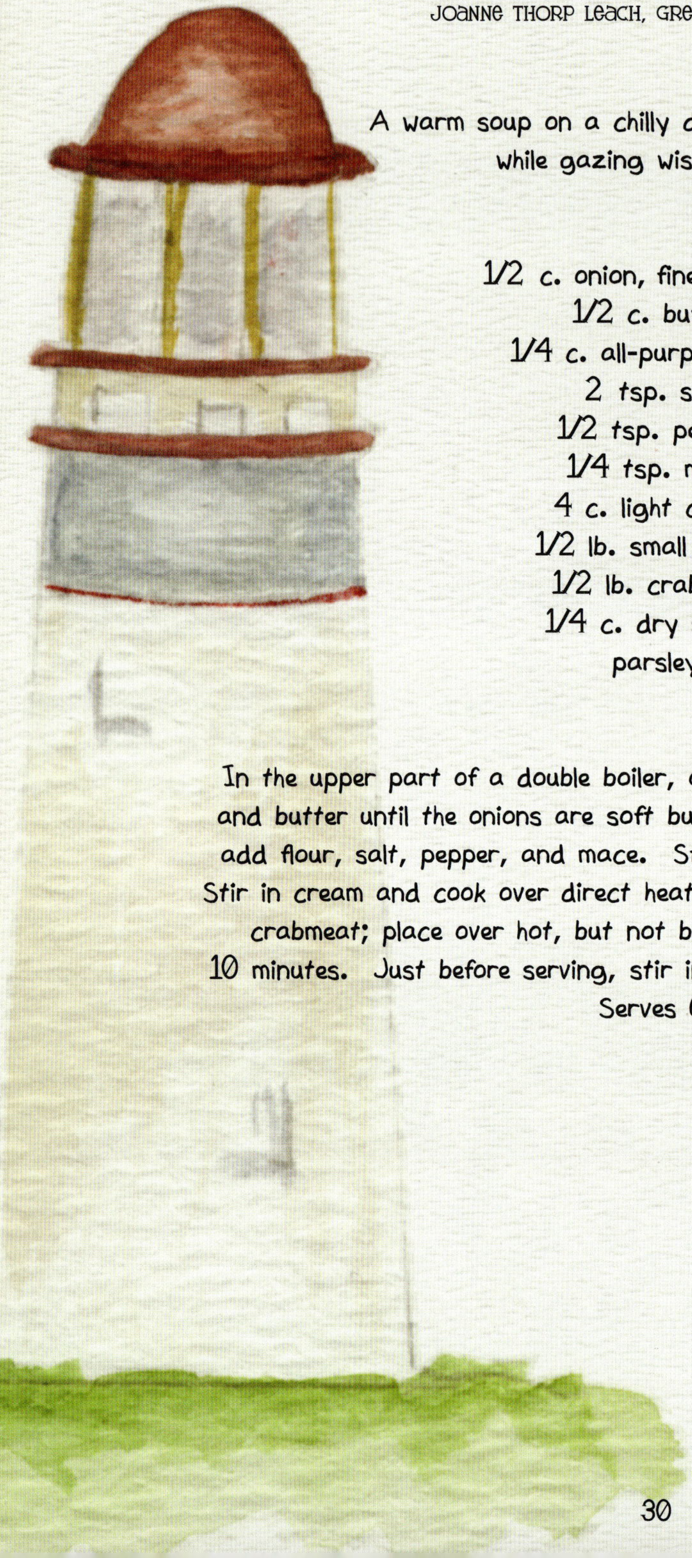

A warm soup on a chilly day, especially tasty if eaten while gazing wistfully at the ocean.

1/2 c. onion, finely chopped
1/2 c. butter
1/4 c. all-purpose flour
2 tsp. salt
1/2 tsp. pepper
1/4 tsp. mace
4 c. light cream
1/2 lb. small shrimp
1/2 lb. crabmeat
1/4 c. dry sherry
parsley

In the upper part of a double boiler, over direct heat, saute the onion and butter until the onions are soft but not brown. Remove from heat; add flour, salt, pepper, and mace. Stir until smooth and well blended. Stir in cream and cook over direct heat until thickened. Add shrimp and crabmeat; place over hot, but not boiling, water. Cook uncovered 10 minutes. Just before serving, stir in sherry. Add parsley for color. Serves 6.

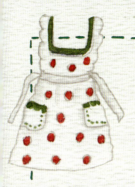

Asparagus Soup Crutee
Christy Bonetti, Monterey, California
(Bib's Granddaughter)

Serve this elegant and delicious soup before a special dinner.

1 quart milk
3 c. chicken stock
1 c. cold water
7 Tbsp. butter
6 Tbsp. flour
2 lbs thin asparagus spears, bottom of stalks trimmed
8 slices French bread
3/4 c. grated Parmesan cheese
white pepper
fresh nutmeg

In a large saucepan, combine milk, stock, and water. Heat to boiling. Set aside. In a 4-quart soup kettle, melt half the butter. Add flour and stir over low heat until flour is cooked and blond. Remove from heat. Whisk in hot milk mixture; add asparagus. Cover and heat to simmering. Set cover ajar and simmer until spears are very soft, about 3 minutes.

Place bread slices on baking sheet. Brush with remaining butter and bake at 400° until lightly browned, turning once. Set aside.

In 2-cup batches, puree cooked asparagus mixture. Return to kettle. Stir in cream and season to taste. Top each bread slice with 2 Tbsp. cheese and melt under a broiled. Serve soup with the crouton on top. Add more cream for thicker and richer soup, if desired. Serves 8.

Veggies and Sidedishes

Bib whistled when she worked, played Pedro, the harmonica and made great beans!

BIB'S BEANS

Nanci Bell, San Luis Obispo, California

Bib was truly famous for two things: her beans and her apple pie. She served these beans at every branding or barbecue on the ranch where I grew up. Neighbors, family, and friends all lined up for Bib's beans.

This is the recipe as Bib told it to me. She often wasn't sure of the exact measurements. She said, "I don't know; about a teaspoon, I guess." So add a heaping teaspoon or a small handful; it probably won't matter.

1 pkg. small pink beans
2 onions, chopped
2 to 3 slices of bacon, chopped
1 lb. hamburger, cooked and drained
2 small cans of "hot sauce," which is really tomato sauce!
1 tsp. salt
dash of pepper
2 tsp. chili powder or Spanish pepper
1 tsp. garlic salt
1 tsp. whole cumin seed, crumbled
(I never put this in, and sometimes my mom didn't either!)
2 tsp. Spice Island bell pepper or any pepper flakes
or put in about 1/2 of a green bell pepper

Fry bacon and onions and then add all the ingredients except beans. Simmer sauce for half an hour. Cook beans according to package instructions. When beans are almost done, add sauce and finish cooking.

CORN CASSEROLE

Heather Kelley, San Luis Obispo, California

This is one of the casseroles that my grandma used to make for the holidays. It has always been one of her favorites. Though Grandma is no longer with us, we have continued the tradition.

6 Tbsp. vegetable oil
1 tsp. garlic salt
2 c. grated sharp cheddar cheese
2 cans creamed corn
2 eggs
1 pkg. Jiffy cornbread muffin mix

Preheat oven to 350° degrees. Mix all ingredients except cheese together in a mixing bowl. Put 1/2 the mixture into a greased baking dish. Cover with 1/2 of the cheese. Put in remaining mixture and cover with the rest of the cheese. Bake at 350° for 30 minutes.

Morristown Sweet Potato Casserole

Mark Ledford, Morristown, New Jersey

This is my personal favorite. This recipe is absolutely delicious. Definitely for those with a sweet tooth.

4 c. cooked mashed sweet potatoes
1 c. sugar
2 large eggs
1 tsp. vanilla extract
1/3 c. milk
1/2 c. butter or margarine, softened
1 c. firmly packed brown sugar
1 c. finely chopped pecans

Beat first six ingredients at medium speed with an electric mixer until smooth. Spoon into a lightly greased 3-quart shallow baking dish. Stir together brown sugar and pecans; sprinkle over the casserole. Bake uncovered at 350° for 30 minutes. Makes 8 to 10 servings.

Rice and Veggie Pie

Julie Hayden, Raymondville, Texas

This is a great recipe to add to your favorite vegetables. You can cook the rice ahead or use leftovers and then assemble the casserole quickly on one of those hectic weeknights. Just add a salad and you've got it made.

1 c. cooked brown rice
3 eggs
1 c. cheddar cheese, grated
1 Tbsp. butter
2 cloves garlic, minced
2/3 c. chopped onion
2/3 c. half and half
salt and pepper to taste
dash or 2 of cayenne pepper
1 c. parmesan cheese, grated
1 c. sliced veggies, such as red peppers, zucchini, broccoli, carrots, or whatever else you would like to throw in!

Stir together rice, 1 egg, and 1 c. cheddar cheese. Press into bottom and sides of 9" pie pan. Saute garlic and onions in butter until tender/crisp. Beat remaining eggs with half and half, salt, pepper, and cayenne pepper to taste. Pour liquid mixture into pie pan over rice crust and sprinkle with parmesan cheese. Bake covered at 350° for 40-45 minutes, or until brown on top and bottom. Serves 6.

Spinach Artichoke Vegetable Casserole

Anne Renz, Salinas, California
(Bib's Granddaughter)

This is a recipe we use at all family dinners. It is great with turkey, ham, fish, beef—anything!

2 pkgs. frozen chopped spinach, thawed
(squeeze juice out and season with garlic salt, salt, and pepper)
2 jars marinated artichoke hearts, chopped finely
1 8 oz. pkg. cream cheese, softened
6 Tbsp. milk or cream
1/4 c. butter or margarine
1/4 c. Parmesan (or more)

Preheat oven to 375° degrees. Layer bottom of casserole with artichoke hearts and then spinach (no need to butter the dish). Beat milk, butter, and cream cheese together and put on top. Then sprinkle with Parmesan cheese. Refrigerate for 6 hours or overnight, or just bake right away! Bake at 375° degrees for 40 minutes.

Chili Relleno Casserole

Anne Renz, Salinas, California
(Bib's Granddaughter)

This recipe is great to serve with a salad for an easy dinner. It can also be served as a great side dish at a barbecue.

1 large can Ortega chilis
1/2 lb. Monterey jack cheese, grated
1/2 lb. cheddar cheese, grated
4 eggs, beaten
2 Tbsp. flour
1 8 oz. can tomato sauce
1/2 tsp. salt
1 13 1/2 oz. can evaporated milk

Remove seeds from chilis. Place a layer of chilis in a 9x13" baking dish. Slice chilis and open out flat. Add all mixed grated cheeses. Top with rest of chilis. Beat egg, add flour, salt, and milk, and mix well. Pour over chilis. Bake at 375° degrees for 30 minutes or until custard is set. Remove from oven and make a lattice design on top with tomato sauce. Bake 5 minutes more and serve. Cut the recipe in half for a small family.

Hawaiian-Style Potatoes

VALARIE JONES, NIPOMO, CALIFORNIA

When we are in Hawaii, which is as often as possible, we always have these potatoes. They are great on a grill or in the oven. Just be prepared to start them early, as all good things take time!

6 large white potatoes, cut into 1/4" slices
6 Maui or sweet onions, thinly sliced
butter
salt and pepper to taste

On a piece of foil, lay 1 cut potato and insert onion slices between every potato slice. Repeat for all the potatoes and onions, then slather with butter and sprinkle salt and pepper to taste. Roll the foil to seal. Grill on a barbecue for 60-90 minutes or bake for 40-60 minutes.

Seven-Layer Salad

Jane Miller, San Luis Obispo, California

This salad is a very simple and lovely addition for a holiday dinner or any special occasion.

Salad:
1 small head lettuce, torn into bite-sized pieces
2 c. celery, finely chopped
1 medium onion, very finely minced
2 c. green pepper, finely chopped
1 lb. pkg. frozen green peas, cooked and cooled
12 to 16 oz. shredded cheddar cheese
1 lb bacon, cut into 1" pieces and then cooked until very crispy, drained

Dressing:
1 1/2 c. mayonnaise
2 to 3 Tbsp. sugar, adjust to taste
2 to 3 Tbsp. milk, adjust to desired consistency
2 tsp. celery seed

In a large deep glass bowl, layer the following ingredients in order: lettuce, celery, onion, green pepper, green peas, cheese, and bacon. Pour dressing on top just before serving. Do not toss!

Weeknight Dinners

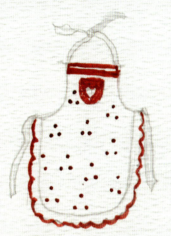

BEEROCKS

MARY LYMAN, SAN LUIS OBISPO, CALIFORNIA

This is a German delight—it's a meal in a roll! My mother-in-law introduced this to me when I first got married. It had been in the family for years and is a great favorite whether eaten hot or cold. It's even good dipped in catsup.

1/4 c. oil in a large pot
1 whole small or medium cabbage, shredded into long shreds
1 pkg. frozen white bread loaves (3 in 1 pkg.)
1 whole onion, finely chopped
2 c. ground roast beef, hamburger, or turkey

Put chopped onion into heated oil and cook until clear. Add cabbage, stirring occasionally. Add salt and pepper to taste. Add cooked meat to cabbage. Let frozen loaves rise and roll out to 1/4" thick. Cut into rectangles. Place a small handful of mixture on one side of the rectangle. Turn over and pinch edges to seal. Place on an ungreased cookie sheet. Let it rise again to half its size. Bake uncovered at 350° until golden brown, approximately for 30 to 45 minutes.

You can vary this recipe to make it vegetarian. Just add water chestnuts, pine nuts, grated carrots, olives...you name it!

Chicken Quesadillas
Christy Bonetti, Monterey, California
(Bib's Granddaughter)

A favorite local restaurant serves this, so I adapted it for an easy dinner or appetizer.

8 10" tortillas
1 chicken breast
2 roasted red bell peppers, sliced
1 avocado, mashed
1/3 c. sour cream
1/4 c. green onions, chopped
1/2 tsp. garlic powder
2 c. smoked gouda or mozzarella cheese
salt and pepper to taste

Mix together avocado, sour cream, green onions, garlic powder, and salt and pepper to taste. Grill the chicken and shred into small pieces when cool. Spread avocado mixture on 4 tortillas. Sprinkle chicken, roasted red bell peppers, and cheese. Cover with remaining tortillas and brown lightly on both sides. Serve with salsa. To roast the bell peppers, put them in a dish in the oven at 350°. Leave in the oven until skin starts to blister. When skin has blistered, throw them in a paper bag and seal. When peppers have cooled, just remove skin. Dungeness crab can be substituted for the chicken.

Easy Taco Chili

Terri Mehl, Sacramento, California

If you want a tasty and healthy meal and also want something you can leave alone with great results, this is a keeper. And, by the way, 1 c. equals 1 Weight Watchers' point!

1 lb. lean ground turkey (97% fat free)
1 onion, chopped
2 to 3 cloves garlic, minced (more if you love it)
1 c. celery, chopped
1 15 oz. can tomato sauce
1 4 oz. can chopped green chilies
1 or 2 15 oz. cans chopped or stewed tomatoes
(Mexican or plain)
4 16 oz. cans beans
(pinto, kidney, black, or mix and match)
1 pkg. taco seasoning
1 pkg. Hidden Valley Ranch Dressing Mix
2 tsp. cumin (can be 3-4 depending on your taste)
16 oz. bag of frozen white corn
1 c. water (optional—it can make the chili soupier)

Brown the turkey, then add onions, garlic, and celery as turkey begins to brown. One by one, add the remaining ingredients. Do not drain anything, just dump! Heat to a nice boil, then simmer to mix the flavors. This recipe can also be made in a crockpot by browning the first 4 ingredients and then dumping it all in the pot. Set on low for 4-6 hours and you are set! Makes 4-6 generous servings.

McCALL'S ALMOST VEGETARIAN CHILI

LIZ McCALL SZPORN, MARIN, CALIFORNIA

Delicious and perfect with corn bread muffins. Just put it on the stove and go relax for awhile!

2 or 3 Tbsp. olive oil
1 each large red, orange, green, and yellow bell pepper, chopped
2 or 3 large Habanera peppers, chopped finely
2 or 3 large Jalapeno peppers, chopped finely
2 ears of corn, kernels cut off
15 oz. can Cannellini beans, drained and rinsed
15 oz. can each black beans and dark red kidney beans
28 oz. crushed tomatoes
15 oz. diced yellow or red tomatoes
15 oz. tomato sauce
2 lb. ground beef or turkey
1 1/2 to 2 1/2 tsp. cumin (to desired taste and spiciness)
5 to 7 Tbsp. chili powder (to desired taste and spiciness)
2 Tbsp. sugar

In a large stock pot, saute onions and garlic in olive oil until tender. Throw in all peppers to saute and soften. In a separate pan, cook ground beef until done, drain juices, and add to stock pot. Add chili powder, cumin, salt, and pepper to taste. Let entire pot simmer for about 4-6 hours. Garnish with shredded cheddar cheese, sour cream, and chopped onions.

Veggie Pasties
Ali Prigg, New York, New York

This recipe was inspired by the *Redwall* series of books by Brian Jacques. These pasties* are perfect for using leftovers or remnants of veggies or meat in the fridge. If using meat in a pasty, sear or brown the meat before putting in the veggies.

Pasties:
1 pkg. refrigerated pie crust * 1/4 c. diced celery
1/2 c. shredded or chopped carrots * 1 clove garlic, chopped
salt and pepper to taste * 4 oz. cream cheese
1 c. shredded sharp cheddar cheese * 1 1/2 c. diced potatoes
1 c. chopped broccoli * 1/2 c. cooked mushrooms
2 Tbsp. olive oil

Gravy:
3 c. vegetable, chicken, or beef broth * 1 Tbsp. butter
1/4 c. flour

For pasties, mix all vegetables and seasonings with olive oil in a large bowl. Keep cheese separate for now. Split each pie crust in half (you should have 4 half circles). Stuff each half circle with vegetable mixture. Top each half with 1 oz. of cream cheese broken into small chunks and 1/4 c. of cheddar cheese. Fold the pie crust and seal tightly. Cut small slits into the dough to vent steam. Bake in a 375° oven for 45 minutes or until golden brown. Serve pasties with gravy on top.

For gravy, melt the butter. Stir in flour until it forms a paste. Warm the broth until steaming, then add the mixture until dissolved and broth is thickened.

* a pasty is like a turnover!

Fish Tacos

Ali Prigg, New York, New York

Great for summer! You can use grouper, tilapia, or just about any other fish that you like.

Marinade:
1 Tbsp. tequila
1 Tbsp. sugar
1 Tbsp. vegetable oil
1 Tbsp. finely chopped Serrano chili, seeded
1-2 Tbsp. cilantro
salt and pepper to taste
1 Tbsp. red wine vinegar
1 red onion, chopped
2-3 Tbsp. limes, juiced
fresh fish fillets or steaks

Dressing:
fat-free sour cream
cilantro
lime juice
salt

Blend above ingredients together. Marinade fish in flat pan in refrigerator for up to 30 minutes. Salt and pepper each side of the fish. After grilling for a few minutes on each side, top fish with chopped fresh chives and a few squeezes of lime. Slice fish into strips or chunks.

Put the fish into your favorite tortilla. You can add shredded cabbage or lettuce, sliced red onion, avocado, salsa, and top with the dressing.

Main Dishes

BIB'S ENCHILADAS

NANCI BELL, SAN LUIS OBISPO, CALIFORNIA

Everyone loved my mom's enchiladas! She served them at barbecues and brandings—and nearly always on Christmas Eve. She'd usually make an additional batch and then freeze it for later.

1 dozen flour tortillas
1 lb. hamburger
6 small onions, chopped
2 lbs. sharp cheese, grated
1 can "hot sauce"
(which turned out to be tomato sauce when I questioned her)
1 can pitted olives
1 large can Las Palmas enchilada sauce

Saute hamburger in oil (or bacon grease, she said!). Remove from skillet, add two tbsp. of salad oil and 2 or 3 tbsp. of flour. Brown as making gravy, also add about a teaspoon of salt.

Add the can of enchilada sauce and small "hot sauce" to flour mixture. If too thick, add a can of water. Simmer while preparing onions and cheese. Cool before dipping tortillas in sauce. Butter a large shallow pan or a few 9x13" pyrex dishes. Dip tortillas in sauce. Lay in pan and add handful of cheese, meat, and small onion, and roll. (Add in chopped ortega chilis as part of the stuffing, or even some chopped hard boiled eggs.) Pour left over sauce over the top of the rolled enchiladas, then sprinkle with remaining cheese and dot with olives. Bake uncovered at 325-350° for 20-30 minutes. Serves 12.

Korean Braised Short Ribs
Kalbi Chim
Jane Miller, San Luis Obispo, California

When I lived in Korea, my friend's mother often made this dish for me. Now her recipe has become a favorite of my friends and family here. The pear juice is a special touch to make the beef especially tender.

1 to 1 1/2 lbs. beef short ribs
3 Tbsp. red wine
3 Tbsp. low sodium soy sauce
2 Tbsp. sugar (more if you prefer a sweeter sauce)
2 Tbsp. garlic, finely minced or ground
2 small green onions, cut into 1" pieces
1 small jar pear juice (in the baby food section of the supermarket, about 1/4 c.)
1 large onion, finely minced or ground
3/4 tsp. black pepper
10 raw chestnuts, peeled (or 2 medium potatoes cut into chunks)
1 Tbsp. pine nuts or walnut pieces (optional)

Soak ribs in cold water for 30 minutes. Drain. Place the ground onion into a cheesecloth and squeeze all the liquid into a large bowl. Do the same with the garlic. Add the pear juice, green onion, wine, black pepper, sugar, and soy sauce to the bowl. Mix well. Place the ribs in the bowl and mix until well coated. Let set for 30 minutes to one hour. Place ribs and sauce in a large heavy pot and cook at medium-high heat until the sauce begins to boil. Reduce heat slightly and cook until sauce reduces to the point where it just covers the bottom of the pan. The ribs should be almost done. Add chestnuts (or potatoes) and walnuts. Cook for about 10 minutes. Stir well, then continue cooking on low heat until ribs are tender, the chestnuts (or potatoes) are done, and the liquid is almost gone. Serve with steamed rice.

CRANBERRY CHICKEN
SHANNON KENDALL, INDIANAPOLIS, INDIANA

This dish reminds me of Thanksgiving. I usually omit the raisins.

8 chicken breasts
2 c. whole cranberry sauce
1/2 c. red wine

Dressing:
2 c.s Pepperidge Farm herb dressing
1/4 c. chopped walnuts
1/4 c. golden raisins, chopped
1/4 tsp. sage, optional
1/4 c. chicken broth
1/4 c. butter, melted
salt and pepper to taste

Mix dressing ingredients together. Lay stuffing in greased casserole dish, then chicken, then cranberry and wine sauce. Bake uncovered at 350° for 1 1/4 hours.

MEATBALLS

Cayce Meade, Newport Beach, California

This recipe comes from my grandmother, Leona Harris, and was published in the Anita, Iowa cookbook.

1/2 c. cornflakes (crushed), can use crushed bread crumbs
1 small onion, chopped
1 clove garlic, crushed
2 eggs, beaten
2 lbs. ground beef
salt and pepper to taste

1 large bottle chili sauce
16 oz. glass of grape jelly
juice of 1 lemon

Mix first six ingredients and form into walnut-sized balls. Combine chili sauce, grape jelly, and lemon juice in a heavy skillet and simmer for five minutes. Place meatballs in sauce. Cook slowly for one hour. Can be frozen. Makes 60 meatballs.

Honey Salmon
Matt Robinson, Santa Barbara, California

This dish comes from my friend's mother (where many other good dishes come from) and she got it from her best friend while she lived in Alaska. Her friend said she considered it the perfect dinner for when it was freezing in the woods around her, she had a good fire inside, and she didn't feel like doing anything in the kitchen.

2 Tbsp. butter
salmon (Alaskan salmon is best)
2 Tbsp. Dijon mustard
4 Tbsp. honey
1/4 c. walnuts or pecans
2 Tbsp. fresh parsley finely chopped
1/4 c. breadcrumbs
salt
pepper

Mix walnuts, breadcrumbs, and parsley. Melt butter. Mix in honey and mustard. Sprinkle salt and pepper over the salmon. Spread butter mixture over the salmon. Put walnut mixture over the fish. Cook at 450° for 10 minutes. per inch of thickness of the salmon.

Mike's Genuine Handmade Sicilian Gnocchi

Mike Kelsey, San Luis Obispo, California

My gnocchi is world-renowned and can only be made with opera playing on the stereo while sipping a glass of red wine.

4 medium potatoes
1 egg
2-3 c. flour
2 Tbsp. salt

Drop medium potatoes into a large pot of boiling water for 45 minutes. Remove, strain, and let cool. Peel and cut into thirds. Using a ricer, which is like an oversized garlic press, squish the potatoes into a large bowl. Dust a large space on your counter with flour.

Make a pile of flour in the center (about two c.). Pour the riced potatoes onto the pile, then cover with about 1/2 c. of flour. Beat the egg into submission. Make a hole into the center of the mound of potatoes and flour and add egg. Sprinkle two Tbsp. of salt over the top of the whole mess and start kneading into a thick dough until all ingredients are combined. Dust with extra flour as needed. Consistency should be like bread dough; not too moist or too dry.

Break off a handful of the dough and roll between your hands to form a cylinder. Place it on the counter and continue rolling until dough is about 3/4" thick. Using a knife, cut the dough diagonally into 3/4" bits. Squish your finger into each piece to make an indention and then place on a lightly floured cookie sheet until all of the dough is used.

Drop bits into a large pot of boiling water until they rise to the surface (3-5 minutes). Strain and top with your favorite sauce. Abondanza!

TARRAGON CHICKEN
ERICA OLSON, DENVER, COLORADO

This is one of my favorite recipes from childhood. My sister and I adored the crunchy skin and would always beg extra from our parents, spooning extra juice over the chicken to soak up in our rice. My mother loved it because it was easy and she could start it in the oven on a timed bake. During the cold Alaskan winters, it was wonderful to come home to the redolent scent that spread throughout the house.

1/4 c. lemon
2 Tbsp. tarragon
1 Tbsp. paprika
1/2 Tbsp. Tabasco
1 tsp. Salt
1 chicken, cut into pieces

Bake uncovered at 350° for one hour, basting the chicken occasionally.

EMPANADAS
Cristina Miller, Crete, Nebraska

I make these empanadas a few times a year. These are not only a favorite of our family, but also of my friends and coworkers!

Filling:
1 lb. lean ground beef
1/2 medium onion, chopped
1/2 medium green pepper, chopped
2 cloves garlic, minced
1 med. tomato, diced
1 small can tomato paste
1 Tbsp. Worcestershire sauce
salt and pepper to taste
1 pinch cayenne pepper or 1 dash Tabasco sauce, if desired

Dough:
(This is a basic pie dough recipe, except use hot water instead of cold)
2 c.s flour
2 tsp. salt
2 c. shortening
2 Tbsp. hot water

In a large skillet, brown beef with onion, green pepper, and garlic. Drain. Add remaining filling ingredients and mix well. Remove from heat.

On a floured surface, roll walnut-sized balls of dough into 3 or 4" diameter circles. Place a small spoonful of meat mixture onto center of each circle. Carefully fold dough over the mixture and fork down the edges to seal. At this point, the empanadas can be frozen in a sealed container lined with waxed paper for up to a few weeks.

In a deep skillet, heat about one inch of oil, then carefully add empanadas. Fry until golden brown. Drain on paper towels and enjoy!

Bib's Italarini

Nanci Bell, San Luis Obispo, California

This was a favorite from Billie Taylor (Bib) at barbecues or brandings. She also served it as a main dish for just a quick family get together.

My sons, Rody and Rhett, stopped by Bib's house every day after school (even when they were in high school). She made them laugh and always had cookies, frosted brownies, or maybe some leftover Italarini waiting in her kitchen.

Whistling as she worked, she'd put the Italarini on the table with French bread and a green salad...and we all loved it. All was right with the world.

1 pkg. of egg noodles
1 can cream corn
1 can pitted olives
1 pound of hamburger
2 cans "hot sauce" (which is really tomato sauce!)
1 tsp salt
a dash each of Spanish pepper, garlic salt, and black pepper
2 small onions, chopped

Saute hamburger and onions, then add hot sauce, olive juice, salt, pepper, garlic salt, and chili powder. Simmer while cooking noodles until almost done. Drain noodles. Add sauce, corn, and olives. Mix in pot. Put in buttered casserole. Sprinkle grated cheese on top. Bake at 350° for approximately 30 minutes.

(May add small can of mushrooms, liquid and all, and some Ortega peppers.)

Bill Bustamante's "Knock Your Socks Off" Mustard Sauce

Alison Bell, San Luis Obispo, California
(Bib's Granddaughter)

Our friend Bill devised this delicious sauce, a perfect dipping sauce for a nice ham. Careful—it can be a little hot!

2 Tbsp. of Coleman's mustard powder
3-4 Tbsp. distilled white vinegar
1 1/2 Tbsp. of brown sugar

You can add lime juice for a nice twist.

Desserts

LEMON SORBET

ALISON BELL, SAN LUIS OBISPO, CALIFORNIA
(BIB'S GRANDDAUGHTER)

California can get very warm in the summer! This sorbet is an easy cool dessert for a warm summer evening.

3 c. boiling water
1 c. sugar
2 tsp. grated lemon rind
1/2 c. frozen lemon juice, thawed

Combine boiling water and sugar in a medium bowl stirring until sugar dissolves; cool. Stir in lemon rind and juice and pour into four tubs or dishes. Freeze until firm.

BIB'S COFFEE-FROSTED BROWNIES

RODY BELL, SAN LUIS OBISPO, CALIFORNIA
(BIB'S GRANDSON)

It was great to visit Bib's house after school, especially for the frosted brownies. It seemed like she made these on a lark one day. While Rhett and I were standing around waiting to lick the beaters and the bowl, she grabbed her coffee pot. Giggling at the look on our faces, she poured some coffee into the frosting! Surprising to us, it turned out great and coffee became a permanent part of the recipe.

your favorite boxed brownie mix
1 can butter cream frosting
or make the frosting from the powdered sugar box
1 small pkg. chocolate chips
jigger of brewed coffee

Mix your favorite brownies and stir chocolate chips into the mix. Bake according to recipe. Cool. Make frosting and then add the jigger of coffee to it. Spread over the top of the cooled brownies. The frosting will be thick and creamy and the brownies will be especially great because they have a layer of melted chocolate on the bottom from the chocolate chips in the mix.

P.S. For something extra special, save some chocolate chips and spell out your favorite grandson's name on the frosting!

Apple Crisp

SHANNON KENDALL, INDIANAPOLIS, INDIANA

My brother asks our mom to bake him an apple crisp every year instead of a birthday cake. It always makes me think of Fall when I smell it baking.

Filling:
4 c. apples, sliced
3/4 c. sugar
1 Tbsp. flour

Topping:
1 c. brown sugar
1 c. regular oats
1 c. all purpose flour
1/2 c. butter
1 tsp. Vanilla

In the bottom of a greased baking pan, put sliced apples, sugar, and flour. Spread topping mixture over this. Bake one hour or longer if necessary at 350° degrees. Try it with ice cream or Ambrosia Devon custard.

PEPPERMINT HOT FUDGE SUNDAES

Lisa Nowell and Ryn Singley, San Francisco, California

Every once in a while, you need to throw out all thoughts of watching your weight and live it up. This is a great way to do that.

1 c. heavy cream
1/3 c. light corn syrup, plus more to adjust consistency
1   12 oz. bag semisweet chocolate chips
1 tsp. peppermint extract
best quality vanilla ice cream
peppermint candy, coarsely chopped

In a small saucepan, combine heavy cream and corn syrup. Stir to combine and bring just to a boil over med-high heat. Remove from heat and add chocolate and peppermint extract. Whisk until chocolate is melted. If necessary, adjust consistency with additional corn syrup. Pour over ice cream and garnish with chopped peppermint candy.

Baked Goods and Sweets

Bib's Crunchy Jumble Cookies

ALISON BELL, SAN LUIS OBISPO, CALIFORNIA
(BIB'S GRANDDAUGHTER)

This is my grandmother's recipe. I still have it on a recipe card in her handwriting—so special to me.
(Of all Bib's grandchildren, Alison spent the most time with her. Bib was her special friend. Nearly everyday after school, while I worked, Alison and Bib sat in her living room and watched Tom and Jerry cartoons together, played cards, laughed...and ate. When reprimanded for feeding Alison so many sweets, Bib didn't hesitate to remind me that we are what we eat, eating is our bodies' fuel, and besides, cookies are good for you!—Nanci)

1 1/4 c. flour
1/2 tsp. baking soda
1/4 tsp. salt
1/2 c. butter
1/2 c. coconut
1 tsp. vanilla
1/2 c. walnuts (optional)
1 egg
1 c. sugar
2 c. Rice Krispies
2 heaping Tbsp. Hershey's cocoa
1 c. chocolate chips

Sift dry ingredients together. Cream butter, sugar, and vanilla until very creamy. Add egg and beat in. Add flour, sugar, baking soda, salt, cocoa, cereal, chocolate chips, coconut, and walnuts. Drop by spoonfuls on cookie sheet. Flatten with fork; dip fork in glass of water often. Bake at 350° for 10-12 minutes.

4th Generation Banana Bread

Nikki Sturtevant, Saratoga, California

Nothing says home like the smell of banana bread baking in the oven! This one is a family favorite for over 100 years, passed down for 4 generations, and is a staple every winter.

1/2 c. shortening or softened butter
1 c. sugar
2 eggs, well beaten
3 bananas, very ripe and mashed
2 c. flour, sifted
1 tsp. baking soda
1/2 tsp. salt
1/2 c. walnuts, chopped (optional)

Sift dry ingredients together and set aside. In a large mixing bowl, mix together butter, sugar, and eggs. Add other dry ingredients and stir well. Add mashed bananas and chopped walnuts, stir. Pour into greased bread pan. Bake on center rack at 350° for 1 hour 15 minutes, but check after 1 hour with a wooden skewer or knife. It should come out clean. If the top is turning very dark, cover loosely with foil to prevent burning. Cool in pan on cooling rack for 1 minute. Remove loaf from pan and cool an additional 10-15 minutes before cutting. Loaf should be moist.

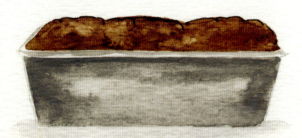

ALMOND GLAZED SUGAR COOKIES

ASHLEY SMITH, MOBILE, ALABAMA

I make these cookies with my mom every Christmas and we give them to friends, family and co-workers.

Dough:
1 c. butter, softened
3/4 c. sugar
1 tsp. almond extract
2 c. flour
1/2 tsp. baking powder
1/4 tsp. salt

Glaze:
1 1/2 c. powdered sugar
1 tsp. almond extract
4-5 tsp. water
Sliced almonds for decoration

Preheat oven to 400°. Combine butter, sugar, and almond extract in a bowl. Beat at medium speed, scraping bowl often, until creamy (1-2 minutes). Reduce speed to low and add all remaining cookie ingredients. Beat until well mixed. Roll dough into 1" balls. Place the balls on a baking sheet 2 inches apart. Flatten the balls to 1/4" thickness with the bottom of a buttered glass dipped in sugar. Bake for 7-9 minutes or until edges are lightly browned. Cool one minute and remove from the cookie sheet. Stir together all glaze ingredients in a small bowl with a wire whisk. Decorate cooled cookies with glaze and sliced almonds. Makes 3 1/2 dozen cookies.

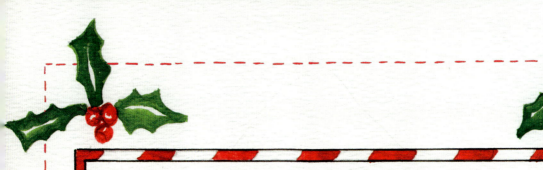

CANDY POPCORN
MARY PELTIER, DENVER, COLORADO

This is a tried and true recipe that is great fun to share with children. Use it as a snack at parties, football games, or anywhere else.

2 c. light brown sugar
2 sticks butter or margarine
1/2 c. light Karo corn syrup
1/2 tsp. baking soda
1 Tbsp. salt
1 Tbsp. vanilla
8 qts. popped popcorn
1 can beer nuts

Boil first 5 ingredients for 5 minutes. Remove from heat and add baking soda, stir. Pour heated mixture onto popcorn and nuts. Stir until popcorn is coated. Bake at 250° for 1 hour...stirring every 20 minutes.

New York Cheesecake

Jane Miller, San Luis Obispo, California

This is wonderful plain or topped with fresh strawberries and drizzled with warm strawberry or raspberry jam.

Shortbread Crust:
1 stick (1/2 c.) butter, well chilled and cut into small pieces
1 1/2 c. flour
1/3 c. sugar
1 egg

Filling:
1 pkg. cream cheese, softened
1 eggs
1 c. sugar
1 c. sour cream or plain yogurt
1 tsp. vanilla or lemon extract
1 c. flour

Preheat oven to 400°. To make the crust, combine the flour and sugar and place into a mound. Form a well in the middle of the mound and break the egg into the well. Place the pieces of butter on the sides of the mound. Using a pastry blender or two knives in a cutting motion, combine the flour mixture and the butter and slowly incorporate the egg. Mix well. Press 1/2 of the dough onto the bottom of a springform pan and bake at 400° for about 10 minutes, or until just slightly brown. Cool. Press remaining dough onto the sides of the pan.
Fill with cheesecake mixture.

Using a sturdy electric mixer, blend the packages of cream cheese and the eggs until soft and fluffy. Add the remaining filling ingredients one at a time, mixing well between each addition. Pour into springform pan. Bake at 400° until the cheesecake rises high and pulls away slightly from the sides of the pan and crust (about 40-45 minutes). Cool completely.

BIB'S APPLE PIE

Nanci Bell, San Luis Obispo, California

Bib was known for her great pie, but especially her fresh apple pie. No canned apples, please. I can still see her in the kitchen. Red curly hair (no matter her age). Hands immersed in the deep bowl. Flour up to her elbows. Rolling pin whizzing and thumping the table, expertly rolling out the dough. Whistling the same unknown tune. She smiled when I first asked her for the recipe...there was no recipe. She started to say, "Well, put about this much flour, and this much salt, and add shortening until it feels right..." We laughed and laughed.

Crust:
2 c. flour * 1 tsp. salt
2/3 c. to a c. shortening * 5 to 6 Tbsp. cold water or 7-Up

Filling:
6 or 7 tart apples, pippins are great * 1 c. sugar
1 to 2 Tbsp. flour * 1 to 1/2 tsp. cinnamon
2 to 3 Tbsp. butter * pinch of salt

Mix flour and salt together. Put shortening into the mixture and mix it with your fingers, flaking it until it feels right (like small little chunks). Gently sprinkle the water around the mixture and form it into a ball with your hands. Put flour on a board or table, break the ball of dough in half, flour hands and rolling pin, and roll the crust. Flour your rolling pin as often as you need to. Put the crust in the bottom of the pie plate, but don't cut off the extra crust.

Pare the apples, slice them, and lay slices in bottom pie crust. Pour the sugar all around the apples, then sprinkle the cinnamon, salt, and flour on top of the apples. Dot with butter.

Roll out the top pie crust and place it on the apples. Place your knife in flour and cut off the extra dough around the edges. Cut pie design on the top crust so it will breath, then put a little cream or milk on your hands and rub it on the top crust. Sprinkle with sugar.

Bake at 400° for 50 minutes.

CARROT CAKE

Christy Bonetti, Monterey, California
(Bib's Granddaughter)

This recipe was given to me by a college friend who has recently passed away. This recipe has special meaning because I think of her when I make it. We used it for our wedding. I imagine the baker hated my choice, because of all of the carrot grating!

Cake:
4 eggs
2 c. sugar
1 c. of flour
2 tsp. baking powder
2 tsp. baking soda
2 tsp. cinnamon
1 tsp. salt
3 c. grated carrots
(1 carrot equals approximately 1/2 c.)
1 8.15 oz. can crushed pineapple

Frosting:
1/2 c. butter
1 lb. powdered sugar
1 8 oz. pkg. cream cheese, softened
1 tsp. vanilla
4 Tbsp. crushed pineapple (optional)

Mix sugar, oil, and eggs, then add the rest of cake ingredients. Bake at 350° for 40 minutes in a greased pan. Combine all frosting ingredients. Beat until fluffy. Fold in pineapple and frost the cake. Makes 2 layers or 1 oblong cake.

BIB'S SUGARED WALNUTS

CHRISTY BONETTI, MONTEREY, CALIFORNIA
(BIB'S GRANDDAUGHTER)

Every Christmas as we arrived at Bib's house for the holidays there was always a bowl of her sugared walnuts on a table filled with bowls of holiday candies and cookies.

(Bib whistled while she worked—a tune none of us had ever heard before or since. Where eating was concerned, everyday was like a HOLIDAY for Bib. She truly believed that all food was good for you.
In high school, Rody and Rhett would go by Bib's house for food. Walking in the door, with a fire crackling in the fireplace, you could smell whatever delight Bib had waiting for them. Some afternoons it was brownies, sometimes it was pies, sometimes cakes, and on a wintery day it might have been her sugar-coated walnuts—Nanci)

2 1/2 c. walnut halves
1 c. sugar
1/2 c. brown sugar
1/2 c. water
1 tsp. cinnamon
1 1/2 tsp. vanilla

Toast walnuts at 375° degrees for about 15 minutes, stirring often. Let cool. Cook sugar, water, and cinnamon until it is at a soft ball stage without stirring. Keep testing for soft balls in cold water. When soft balls form between your fingers, remove from heat. Add vanilla, then nuts while stirring gently until mixture becomes creamy or turns to sugar. Turn out on wax paper and separate quickly.

ABSURD CHOCOLATE CAKE
TERRI MEHL, SACRAMENTO, CALIFORNIA

A little vinegar in the recipe makes this cake a little absurd!

3 c. flour
2 c. sugar
2 tsp. baking soda
1 tsp. Salt
6 Tbsp. cocoa powder (unsweetened)
1 c. corn oil
2 c. water
2 Tbsp. white vinegar
1 tsp. vanilla

Mix dry ingredients in a bowl. Add all the liquids and mix well. Pour into one oblong or two round pans. Bake at 350° for 30-40 minutes. Frost or top with whipped cream or powdered sugar and fresh raspberries.

POPPYSEED CAKE

CORNELIA FLETCHER, ATLANTA, GEORGIA

This is sooooo delicious.

Cake:
1 box Duncan Hines yellow cake mix
1 small pkg. vanilla instant pudding
4 eggs
3/4 c. oil
1 c. sherry (real sherry, not cooking sherry)
1/4 c. poppy seeds

Frosting:
1 stick butter, melted
2 Tbsp. sherry
confectioner's sugar to make desired consistency

Mix together cake ingredients and bake in a tube pan bake at 350° for 45-50 minutes.
Melt butter, stir in sherry, then slowly mix in confectioner's sugar to make desired consistency. Mix carefully to avoid lumps.

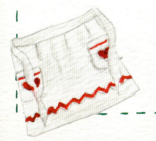

TEXAS SHEET CAKE
Patty Biles, Dallas, Texas

The Lone Star State

This is a traditional Texas recipe that is quick, easy, and delicious.

Cake:
2 c. flour
2 c. sugar
1/2 c. Hersey's cocoa
1/4 tsp. salt
1 Tbsp. vanilla
2 eggs, lightly whisked
3/4 c. vegetable oil
3/4 c. buttermilk
1 tsp. baking soda

Brown Sugar Glaze:
1 1/2 c. brown sugar
1/4 c. butter
dash salt
1/4 c. and 2 Tbsp. milk

Place all cake ingredients in one bowl, sprinkling soda on top. Pour one c. boiling water over the mixture and blend together. Pour into greased 9x13" pan. Bake at 350° degrees for 35-40 minutes.

Mix brown sugar glaze ingredients together and boil for one minute. Poke lots of holes in the cake with a toothpick and pour glaze over cake while cake is still warm.

JEWISH APPLE CAKE

SUSANNE SAFAVI, PHILADELPHIA, PENNSYLVANIA

My mom made this recipe all the time when I was growing up and it turned out to be great for any occasion. Some people even think it's perfect for breakfast the day after.

5-6 apples, peeled, cored, and sliced
2 tsp. cinnamon
2 c. sugar
3 c. flour
1 tsp. baking powder
1 c. oil
1 c. orange juice
4 eggs
1 Tbsp. vanilla

Mix apples with two tsp. cinnamon and five Tbsp. of sugar and set aside. In another bowl, mix the remaining ingredients. Spray a tube cake pan with a non-stick spray. Pour a layer of batter, a layer of apples, a layer of batter, and a layer of apples. Bake at 350° for 60 minutes on the middle shelf until golden brown.

BUTTERSCOTCH BROWNIES
Mary Lyman, San Luis Obispo, California

Here is a nice twist on the traditional brownie. This is a recipe my mother and I made when I was growing up. It's easy and sure to make people smile!

1/4 c. butter
3/4 c. light brown sugar
1 tsp. baking powder
1/2 tsp. salt
1 egg
1/2 tsp. vanilla
1/2 c. coarsely chopped walnuts

Melt the butter over low heat. Remove from heat and stir in brown sugar. Cool butter and sugar and then add flour, baking powder, and salt. Next stir in egg, vanilla, and nuts.

Spread in a well-greased 8" square pan. Bake at 350° for 20-25 minutes or, until when touched lightly with finger, only a slight imprint remains. Cut bars while still warm.

Leona's Cheese Pie

Laurie King Rossi, San Luis Obispo, California

You have to let this set in the refrigerator over night. My mom made this the night before and you could smell it throughout the house as you waited for it. It was special!

Crust:
Roll enough graham crackers to make 2 c. crumbs
(or buy box of graham cracker crumbs)
1/2 c. sugar
1/2 c. melted butter

Filling:
2 8 oz. packages cream cheese, softened
2/3 c. sugar
2 eggs

Topping:
1 c. sour cream
2 Tbsp. sugar
1 tsp. vanilla

Mix graham cracker crumbs with 1/2 c. each sugar and melted butter. Press into the bottom and up the sides of 9" springform pan to form a crust. Now cream the cream cheese until smooth, and blend in eggs, sugar, and vanilla.

Pour into crust and bake for 375° for 20 minutes. Remove from oven and let stand 15 minutes. Combine sour cream, 2 Tbsp. sugar, and vanilla. Carefully spread over baked filling. Return to oven at 425° and bake for 10 minutes. Cool pie and chill overnight. Enjoy!

Breakfast Goodies

The early bird catches the worm

Pat's Cornmeal and Wheatgerm Pancakes

Pat Lindamood, San Luis Obispo, California

These pancakes are very nutritious. Adults often comment that after having these for breakfast, they notice no need for a midmorning snack, and in fact lunchtime may even come and go without their notice. Children who have been known as picky eaters mutually love these pancakes and will often prefer to just hold one and eat without any topping. A syrup topping is, of course, good. Our family prefers a fresh fruit topping like pureed fresh or frozen apricots or applesauce.

4 eggs
1 qt. buttermilk
2 2/3 c. cornmeal
1 2/3 c. wheatgerm
4 Tbsp. flour
2 tsp. baking powder
2 tsp. baking soda
3 Tbsp. sugar
3 Tbsp. cooking oil
1 tsp. salt

Beat the eggs and add buttermilk. Combine the dry ingredients and add to the liquid mixture. Stir in the cooking oil last. Then drop onto the griddle or pan to form pancakes.

HOLIDAY MORNING FRENCH TOAST

JODY ADAMS, CHARLOTTE, NORTH CAROLINA

I found this recipe in the paper a few years ago. It's a sure way to get everyone in the holiday spirit. What I like best is that you can prepare it the night before and then just pop it in the oven in the morning while you're still in your pajamas!

1 c. brown sugar
1/2 c. butter, melted
3 tsp. ground cinnamon, divided
3 tart apples peeled, cored, and thinly sliced
1/2 c. dried cranberries or raisins
1 loaf French bread, cut into 1 inch slices
6 large eggs
1 1/2 c. milk
1 Tbsp. vanilla extract

Combine brown sugar, butter, and 1 tsp. cinnamon in a 9x13" baking dish. Add apples and cranberries, toss to coat. Spread apple mixture evenly over the bottom of the baking dish. Arrange slices of bread on top. Mix eggs, milk, vanilla, and remaining 2 tsp. cinnamon until well blended. Pour mixture over bread, soaking bread completely. Cover and refrigerate 4-24 hours. Bake, covered with aluminum foil, in a preheated 375° for 40 minutes. Uncover and bake five minutes. Remove from oven and let stand five minutes. Serve warm!

BRUNCH CASSEROLE
RHONDA ACHILLES, SAN LUIS OBISPO, CALIFORNIA

This has been a traditional Christmas morning breakfast in my family for many years. It's a great recipe if you are feeding quite a few. Sometimes I will spice it up and add a can of diced green chilis.

1 lb. bulk pork sausage
1/4 lb. chopped mushrooms
1 medium yellow onion, diced
6 large eggs
3 Tbsp. sour cream
1 12 oz. jar mild red salsa
2 c. grated cheddar cheese
2 c. grated mozzarella cheese

Preheat oven to 400° degrees and spray a 9x13" baking dish. In a skillet on medium heat saute sausage, mushrooms, and onions until sausage is browned. Drain and set aside. Place eggs and sour cream in a blender and mix for 1 minute. Pour blended eggs into sausage mixture, stir well, and pour into baking dish. Bake for 5-7 minutes or until eggs are softly set. Remove from oven, spoon salsa over the eggs, and then layer with cheese. Bake at 325° for 30 minutes.

Pumpkin Pancakes
with candied pecans

Ali Prigg, New York, New York

This is great to serve when you have friends or relatives for the weekend.

2 c. pecan halves
2 Tbsp. pure maple syrup, more for drizzling
3 Tbsp. superfine sugar
1 tsp. baking powder
1/2 tsp. salt
1/2 tsp. baking soda
1 1/2 c. flour
2 large eggs
1 1/2 c. buttermilk
1 15 oz. can pumpkin puree
1 tsp. vegetable oil

Place pecans in a large dry skillet over medium heat. Stir until lightly toasted. Spoon syrup on top and stir until coated. Remove from heat. In a large bowl, whisk together eggs and buttermilk. Add pumpkin puree. Add flour mixture and whisk until smooth. Heat a heavy skillet coated with oil and cook pancakes. Place pancakes on warm plates. Garnish with pecans and drizzle with maple syrup.

GRANDMA'S CINNAMON ROLLS

Jane Miller, San Luis Obispo, California

My grandmother was a typical Midwestern farm wife and an incredible baker. Whenever people came to the farm to visit, they would often ask my grandmother for some of her signature cinnamon rolls. To this day, it is rare for anyone to mention my late grandmother without also mentioning her cinnamon rolls.

Dough:
1/4 c. milk * 1/4 c. plus 1 Tbsp. sugar
1/2 tsp. salt * 3 Tbsp. butter
1 pkg. yeast * 1/4 c. warm milk or cream (105 to 115 degrees)
2 1/4 c. flour * 1 egg

Filling:
1/4 to 1/3 c. butter, cut into small pieces
2/3 to 3/4 brown sugar * 1/2 c. milk
1/2 c. water * 1/4 tsp. salt
2 tbsp. butter, melted

Combine 1/4 c. milk, 1/4 c. sugar, salt, and 3 Tbsp. butter in a saucepan. Heat until butter melts (105-115 degrees). In a large bowl, dissolve yeast and 1 Tbsp. sugar in warm water. Let stand 10 minutes. Stir in milk mixture, 1 1/2 c. flour, and egg. Beat until smooth. Stir in remaining flour. Turn dough out on a lightly floured surface. Knead until smooth and elastic (about 8 minutes). Place in a well-greased bowl, turning to grease all sides. Cover and let rise in a warm place free from drafts for about 1 hour. Dough will not quite double in size. Punch dough down. Place about 1/2 of the butter pieces onto the bottom of an 8" square baking pan. Sprinkle 1/4 to 1/3 c. brown sugar and about 1/4 tsp. cinnamon on the bottom of the pan. Turn the dough out on lightly floured surface.

Roll to a 12x8" rectangle. Place butter pieces on the dough. Sprinkle remaining brown sugar, cinnamon, and raisins (optional) on the dough. Roll jelly-roll fashion starting with the long side. Pinch the seam to seal (do not pinch the ends). Cut roll into 1" slices. Place the slices, cut-side down, in the baking pan. Pour warm milk or cream onto the slices. Cover and let rise for 40 minutes to one hour. The rolls will not quite double in size. Bake at 350° for 35-45 minutes. Turn over onto serving dish immediately after removing from the oven. Wait a few minutes before removing pan from top of cinnamon rolls.

Apricot Crepes

Mary Peltier, Denver, Colorado

This is a great recipe for making ahead of time. Just store the crepes and sauce separately in the refrigerator. When you are ready to serve, pour the sauce of the crepes, and warm just before serving.

Sauce:
2/3 c. sugar   *   2 Tbsp. corn starch
1 dash salt   *   2 tsp. lemon juice
1 12 oz. can of apricot nectar

Crepes:
1 c. all-purpose flour
2 eggs   *   1/2 c. milk
1/2 c. water   *   1/4 tsp salt
2 Tbsp. butter, melted

In a large mixing bowl, whisk together the flour and the eggs for the crepes. Gradually add in the milk, water, salt, and butter; beat until smooth. Heat a lightly oiled frying pan over medium high heat. Scoop the batter onto the griddle, using 1/4 c. for each crepe. Cook the crepe for about two minutes, until the bottom is light brown. Loosen with a spatula, turn, and cook the other side. Cool and then roll one thin slice of ham in one crepe and place (touching) in a greased casserole dish. Cook sauce over medium heat until clear. Pour over crepes and place apricot halves on top of the crepes. Warm in 350° oven for about 20-30 minutes.

CHAFING DISH BRUNCH
Cornelia Fletcher, Atlanta, Georgia

There are times for dieting and then there are times when you must throw all caution to the wind! This recipe is delicious and should not be passed up because of the calories.

1 jar pressed dried beef (rinse and pat dry, otherwise it will be too salty)
1 pkg boneless skinned chicken breasts
1/2 lb. mild sausage, rolled into bite-size balls
1/2 lb. bacon, cut into bite-size pieces
1 can undiluted mushroom soup
1 8 oz. carton sour cream
1 small jar pimientos
1 can water chestnuts, sliced

Cut beef and chicken into bite-size pieces. Mix sausage and bacon in 9x11" Pyrex dish. Do not add any seasonings. Bake at 350° for 30 minutes. Mix together mushroom soup and sour cream. Fold in pimientos and water chestnuts. After baking, the meats will be stuck together. Break up and mix with the above mixture. Continue baking for another 30 minutes. Serve on toast points or in pastry shells.

INDEX

Absurd Chocolate Cake	78
Almond Glazed Sugar Cookies	72
Apple Crisp	66
Apricot Crepes	91
Artichoke Dip	10
Artichoke Nibbles	15
Asparagus Bundles	13
Asparagus Soup Crutee	31
Banana Bread	71
Beerocks	44
Bib's Apple Pie	75
Bib's Beans	34
Bib's Coffee-Frosted Brownies	65
Bib's Crunchy Jumble Cookies	70
Bib's Enchiladas	52
Bib's Italarini	60
Bib's Sugared Walnuts	77
Bill Bustamante's Mustard Sauce	61
Brunch Casserole	88
Butterscotch Brownies	82
California-Style Guacamole	11
Candy Popcorn	73
Carrot Cake	76
Chafing Dish Brunch	92
Chicken Salad with Poppy Seeds	20
Chicken Quesadilla	45
Chili Relleno Casserole	39
Chinese Chicken Salad	18
Corn Casserole	35
Cranberry Chicken	54
Easy Taco Chili	46
Empanadas	59
Fish Tacos	49
Grandma's Cinnamon Rolls	90

Hawaiian-Style Potatoes	40
Holiday Morning French Toast	87
Honey Salmon	56
It's Not Your Mother's Spinach Salad	21
Italian Sausage and Tortellini Soup	27
Jan's Veggie Soup	29
Jewish Apple Cake	81
Kevin's Salmon Spread	12
Korean Braised Short Ribs	53
Lemon Sorbet	64
Leona's Cheese Pie	83
McCall's Almost Vegetarian Chili	47
Meatballs	55
Mike's Genuine Handmade Sicilian Gnocchis	57
Morristown Sweet Potato Casserole	36
New York Cheesecake	74
Old-Fashioned Crockpot Chicken Soup	28
Pat's Cornmeal and Wheatgerm Pancakes	86
Peppermint Hot Fudge Sundaes	67
Poppyseed Cake	79
Pumpkin Pancakes with Candied Pecans	89
Raspberry Jello Salad	23
Rice and Veggie Pie	37
Salad Nicoise	19
Seven Layer Salad	41
Shrimp Chowder	30
Spinach and Artichoke Vegetable Casserole	38
Taco Soup	26
Tarragon Chicken	58
Texas Sheet Cake	80
Veggie Pasties	48
Wendy's In-A-Hurry Appetizer	14
Whooten Family Cranberry Salad	22